This Book Belongs to:

_____

From:

_____

Date:

_____

My ABC Career Book

Author: Lillian R. Billups
Editor: Anjeanette Alexander
Illustrator: Shivendra Singh (Digital Art Studioo)
Publication Services: Kingdom News Publication Services, LLC.

DISCLAIMER
All the material contained in this book is provided for educational and informational purposes only. No responsibility can be taken for any results or outcomes resulting from the use of this material.

While every attempt has been made to provide information that is both accurate and effective, the author does not assume any responsibility for the accuracy or use/misuse of this information.

Printed in the United States of America.
ISBN 978-1955127998

My ABC Career Book

By Lillian R. Billups
Illustrations by Shivendra Singh

Lillian and her cousins were playing. She looked at the three girls and said, "Wow, each of you is growing up so quickly! Before you know it, you will have to decide what you want to do when you become adults. You may need to spend a little time exploring your options, but you will find a career you like, which fits your personality, brings you joy, and lets you help others."

Lisa got excited and said, "Let's create a list of careers."
Anna said, "We should find one for every letter of the alphabet."

 is for Accountant.

Accountants handle financial documents for companies and people. They help us keep track of how much money is coming in and going out. Anna quickly said, "I love numbers. I may like this one!"

B is for Baker.

Nina said, "Bakers make pastries for us." Lisa and Anna nodded their heads in agreement and they thought about all the tasty treats they loved to eat.

C is for Carpenter.

"Lisa, do you know what carpenters do?" Lillian asked.
"Yes, carpenters make furniture for our homes,"
replied Lisa. Lillian agreed, "They sure do!"

is for Doctor.

Doctors help us to get well. "I wanna be a doctor, " said Anna. Nina said, "Yes, it would be cool to come up with cures and help save lives."

E is for Engineer.

Lillian said to the girls, "Engineers design machines and software." Lisa said, "They also think about how to keep people and the environment safe with their designs."

F is for Firefighter.

Nina quickly exclaimed, "Firefighters protect us, save our lives, and rescue pets from danger. My friend's mother is a firefighter."

G is for Gardeners.

Gardeners grow beautiful flowers and delicious produce.
Lisa said, "Oh! This sounds like a fun career, but what if I see a
worm? I would probably want to keep all the worms as pets!"

H is for Hairstylist.

"Hairstylists make our hair look amazing," said Lillian. "They sure do," responded Nina. "When I was a flower girl for my cousin's wedding, the hairstylist came and made all our hair look amazing!"

I is for Ice Cream Maker.

Ice cream makers make tasty ice cream. Anna giggled and said, "This sounds like the best career ever. I love ice cream." Nina quickly replied, "I would eat it up before it gets to my customers."

 is for Journalist.

Journalists write true stories for news sources
and keep us informed and updated.
Lisa said, "It would be fun to be on TV every night."

is for Kindergarten Teacher.

Kindergarten teachers help children fall in love with learning.
Lisa said with excitement, "I remember my kindergarten teacher
She was my favorite teacher ever! She read to us while we
sat in a circle on the carpet."

L is for Librarian.

Librarians help us find the books we want and need.
"We have to remember to be quiet at the library," Lillian shushed
the girls. Then, all four broke out into giggles.

M is for Massage Therapist.

Massage therapists help us to relax and relieve stress. Nina squealed and said, "My mommy really likes to relax and get massages."

N is for Nurse.

Nurses help heal patients. Anna stated, "Nurses are super important! Our school nurse makes sure I always have my inhaler at school."

O is for Optometrist.

Optometrists are eye doctors who determine if we need glasses or not. Lisa said, "I had to look at all those letters of many sizes as my optometrist placed them on the wall. I told her which ones I could see." Nina said, "Yes! I remember when we did an eye exam at school." Lillian replied "You are right, Nina. Getting your eyes checked is a health screening."

is for Police Officer.

Police officers make sure we are safe.
"My grandma was a police officer for over twenty years.
She still loves to help and protect people," Anna said.

Q is for Quality Inspector.

Quality inspectors make sure all products meet expectations. Lillian said, "They make sure everything is made in an excellent way so people are pleased with the products they buy."

R is for a Receptionist.

Receptionists greet us when we visit businesses, schools, and hotels. Nina said, "The receptionists at my school always has a kind, warm smile and she knows EVERYTHING."

S is for Songwriter.

Songwriters write songs for movies and TV shows. Lisa began to sing, "All of the - " Anna and Nina waved their hands and covered their ears. "No, Lisa. Songwriters write the songs, not sing them," they complained.

T is for Therapist.

Therapists help us solve challenging social, emotional, or physical problems. Lillian said, "There are different types of therapists. Do you know what they are?""One can help us with our bodies. My mom went to one when she was in a really bad car accident," said Nina. Lisa answered after her. "Some can help us with how we think, feel, or behave." Lillian smiled and said, "Very good, girls! All therapists want to help us be at our best."

is for Usher.

Ushers direct us to our seats at events. Anna said, "My teacher is always telling my class to get into their seats before the bell rings." "I do not think ushers work at schools," Lisa said. "You might see an usher at a play, the movies, a concert, at a sporting event, or even in a church."

is for Veterinarian.

Veterinarians are doctors who care about animals.
Lillian said, "Veterinarians make sure our pets are healthy
and get the proper immunizations to protect them."

W is for Writer.

Writers write stories, movies, plays, and musicals. Nina said, "I think being a writer is exactly the right career for me. Creating different characters and make-believe places would be fun."

is for X-ray Technician.

X-ray Technicians prepare the x-ray machine to examine the skeletal system of our bodies. Anna said, "An x-ray technician looked at my brother's arm when he sprained it during a soccer game." Lillian said, "X-ray technicians are here to help us just like other health care professionals."

is for Yoga Instructor.

Yoga instructors teach us how to use yoga and help us relax. Nina asked, "How do they get their bodies to move in those different positions?" Lisa said, "It looks painful, not relaxing. I would get stuck."

Z is for Zookeeper.

Zookeepers maintain the health and well-being of the animals in the zoo. Anna said, "I love to see the giraffes. They look so graceful when they walk around eating the leaves."

Lillian said, "Well, girls, you have come up with a great list of careers.
Now I have one question for you. . .
"Which one will you choose?"

31

The End!

~~~~~~~

I think I want to be a

_____

because

_____

Made in the USA
Monee, IL
21 May 2023

33864345R00021